The Best Composting Toilet Book Ever Written

We're Not Shitting You!

A Guide to Choosing the Right Composting Toilet

by Cory Eckert

For More Info, Visit - ShopTinyHouses.com

TABLE OF CONTENTS

Introduction

For those of us who take advantage of modern advancements in personal hygiene and waste management, it might be a shock to learn that running water isn't available everywhere. You might not always have access to a septic tank or sewer system. And depending on who you ask, flush toilets are considered an environmental disaster by a growing list of environmentalists as the water crisis continues.

Truth be told, modern waste management systems are what they are today, for a few reasons. Reason one, mixing human waste into large amounts of water makes it much easier to transport from remote locations such as individuals homes to a central facility or waste treatment plant. Reason two, to overcome people's "Ick" response to their own waste. Both reasons are worthy issues to solve but in doing so, society has created a much larger set of issues.

Issue one, mixing human waste with water creates sewage. Yep, human waste isn't sewage until you turn it into that foul smelling, disease breeding soup by mixing it with water.

Issue two, in order to maintain this new system to avoid the "Ick" factor, each household is wasting thousands of gallons of water every single year just to create sewage for someone else to deal with.

Issue three, creating sewage by mixing human waste with water, makes human waste smell exponentially worse than it should.

And last but not lease, issue four, treating sewage to make it safe for the environment is a much more expensive process than treating human waste in its original form.

While there has been a solution to these issues for several decades, it's only been over the past 10 years or so that these solutions (composting toilets), are becoming more and more mainstream. Largely in part to a growing RV, Off-Grid, and Tiny home crowd who have no access to modern plumbing systems, composting toilets are beginning to gain in popularity and become more widely accepted.

CHAPTER 1 - What is a Composting Toilet?

In short, a composting toilet is a human waste management system for use when traditional sewer or septic systems are not available or practical.

The toilet we all know and love, the modern flush toilet, hasn't changed much since it was invented in the 1700's. Water flushes human waste out of the toilet bowl and carries the waste somewhere else. For most people, that somewhere else is the municipal sewer treatment plant by way of city sewer systems that cost hundreds of thousands of dollars to develop, install, and maintain. For those living in rural or remote locations, the water from flush toilets carries waste into a septic tank that must be pumped out every few years.

But for those without access to municipal sewer hookups, or the ability to build a septic system, the composting toilet is the answer. The composting toilet is a 100% green and environmentally safe way to dispose of human waste. The process is simple and completely natural. If you've ever used a garden composter, then you're already familiar with how this works.

Think of composting toilets as the modern version of an outhouse. It eliminates the need to dig a hole, move the outhouse periodically, or deal with foul smells and pests that are all too common in an outhouse. Rather than depositing waste (solids and liquids) into a hole in the ground, then burying the hole and moving the outhouse, composting toilets break down human waste, evaporate or at least separate the liquids, and naturally decompose the waste back into a usable, nutrient rich compost.

Have you ever heard the old phrase "Do Bears S**T in the Woods"? What do you suppose happens to that "S**T"? If you guessed that nature takes care of it and it breaks down naturally, you'd be right! Composting toilets are simply specially designed environments that promote very quick, very natural decomposition of human waste.

Human waste is over 90% water, so a large part of what a composting toilet does, is separate the liquids from the solids. By doing so, the solid waste left over shrinks considerably and leaves behind very little waste to deal with.

Removing the water happens in different ways depending on the type of composting toilet in question. Some toilets separate the liquids from the solids before they ever mix while some separate inside the storage container and evaporate off the remaining liquids. In either case, what's left is a very small amount of relatively dry solid waste that can now be decomposed by natural anaerobic decomposition.

Once fully decomposed, this material is nontoxic and safe to handle, as all the pathogens and viruses you would normally find in human feces is killed off by decomposition process.

What you have left is this nutrient-rich material (compost) you can then use in your landscaping garden or around the base of trees to help aid their growth and development. It's worth noting, most composting toilet manufacturers still recommend that you not put compost toilet waste into a vegetable garden.

The Pros of Owning a Composting Toilet

To the unprepared mind, a composting toilet might sound like a gross thing. We've been conditioned to accept the modern standard of using water to flush waste as the only sanitary way to dispose of it. But allow us the opportunity to share with you the pros of owning a composting toilet, as it's a lot different than you might think (and what you might be used to).

1) You will never again worry about a clogged toilet. There's nothing to flush, so there are no pipes for waste to get stuck in. You won't even need to own a plunger. When you look at the typical toilet, the bowl is large enough for everything to get in, but then compacts it to fit through the pipes, sometimes resulting in a clog and all kinds of stains and messes left behind on the porcelain. That's not how composting toilets operate, so there's never a clog.

2) No more splashing/noises. If you've ever been embarrassed to use the bathroom because of the sounds the water makes, worry no more! Composting toilets are dry, so there is virtually no sound when you go. And naturally, no water means no splash and no loud flushing noises that can be embarrassing.

Composting toilets do a great job at separating the urine from the solid waste, but that also means most of the bathroom duties will require you to sit down to ensure that all the waste is collected and sent where it's meant to go. We'll dig more into how each toilet handles different types of waste later in this book.

3) There is no foul odor. When people first hear about the concept of composting toilets, most assume it would stink up the house, and they don't. In fact, there is very little odor at all, and what little odor you do get is similar to the smell of wood or mulch. Later in this book, I will reveal to you the three biggest reasons why odors are minimized.

4) Water conservation. The average toilet today uses about 1.6 gallons, thanks to advancements in low-flush technology. Older toilets can use as many as 7 gallons. Can you imagine how many gallons of clean drinking water per day a family of four uses just to flush waste? That's in one house, but imagine millions of homes in a single city, all flushing various times per day. All that water and waste is pushed through to a waste processing plant, where chemicals are used to clean the water and the cycle starts over.

The average person uses 7,665 gallons of water each year, so you can start to see how the gallons add up over the period of a lifetime. Just one composting toilet in a single household can help save over 30,000 gallons of clean drinking water each year. Not only will this decision help you make an immediate impact environmentally, but in your wallet as well.

5) The cleanup is easier. Listen, if you don't have splashing around, there's no clogs, and the entire system is designed differently, that means your bathroom is much more sanitary than with your average flush toilet. There will be no need for scrubbing brushes and harmful chemicals. Most users just use a little vinegar, water, and paper towel to clean.

Overall, compost toilets are cleaner, greener, and safer than a flush toilet. We will explain these points in depth as this guide goes along.

Now, let's talk about how it all works.

CHAPTER 2 - How Does a Composting Toilet Work?

Composting toilets work by using a perfect balance of heat, oxygen, moisture, and organic material to effectively create an ecosystem inside the toilet that will turn human waste into nutrient rich compost. By creating a perfect environment for natural decomposition, composting toilets are able to quickly and safely break down waste and transform it into a useable product.

There are three essential functions of a composting toilet that all true compost toilets share. While different brand, make and models of toilets may approach these three fundamental functions differently, the core three functions are always the same, evaporate the moisture, break down solid waste without odor, and produce compost that is safe to handle.

Let's dig a little deeper into each of the three core functions.

1. Evaporate the Moisture

Typically, 90% of human waste is composed of water and will evaporate quickly on its own. Some units have a separate waterless urinal that allows much of the liquid to skip the composting chamber entirely and evaporate more quickly or be removed manually.

In most cases, a vent system allows the liquid waste to evaporate through the vent into the outside air.

More modern systems often have a small heating element or plate to aid in the evaporation process and speed things up. It's important to note that while evaporation of the liquid waste is an important part of the process, a healthy compost toilet should never be completely dry. The decomposition process requires some moisture to complete.

Most modern compost toilets are very good at self-managing the decomposition environment and moisture is very rarely a problem.

2.   Break Down Solid Waste Without Odor

While human waste (including toilet tissue) would eventually break down on its own if left to do so, the process would take much to long and potentially produce some undesirable odors if the environment became too saturated with moisture. In the case of a composting toilet, if left to break down naturally without the modern systems, your house might get the worst of the smell! Modern composting toilets on the other hand takes care of this issue nicely.

A properly operating compost toilet requires the addition of an added material referred to as bulking material. Bulking material is simply peat moss, sawdust, popcorn, or some other additive and in most systems, is periodically mixed with the waste with a crank handle or automatic mixing mechanism.

The purpose of the added bulking material is to mix with the waste, allowing proper aeration of the compost pile. This allows oxygen to pass through the decomposing waste and significantly speed the decomposition process and helps to ensure the finished compost is safe to handle.

By properly venting and aerating the compost inside the toilet, an almost completely odorless process is carried out from start to finish.

Did you cringe when I said "almost odorless"? Don't worry! What little odor there is, is usually a smell similar to sawdust or wood shavings and is not unpleasant at all.

Some creative compost toilet veterans even add used coffee grounds to their systems after making coffee each morning. This not only acts as a good additive to the bulking material, but adds a bit of "Good" smell to the toilet!

Now that we know a little more about the breakdown process, let's dig a little deeper into the smell issue!

When you first hear about a composting toilet that doesn't flush, you might immediately think about it being nothing more than a porta-potty inside the house. If you've ever been inside of one, then you know how horrible the stench can be, as well as being quite unsanitary. That is not the experience you'll have with a composting toilet, I promise, and there are three important reasons why.

Reason #1: Negative pressure. Most modern composting toilet systems include an exhaust fan. Every time you open the lid to do your business, air is sucked in through the toilet, through the tank, and out through a vent, causing a very small negative pressure inside the toilet storage area. It's a lot like turning on the bathroom fan, except the fan is inside the tank and doesn't allow the odors to escape.

Reason #2: Bacteria. There are various types of bacteria. As humans, we have bacteria in our gut that help us digest food and keep us healthy (or can make us sick). These bacteria can produce very foul odors and gas (sulfur).

Some composting toilet companies will provide you with a packet of microbes that you put into the tank along with the bulking agents. When you manipulate the ecosystem of the tank, it breeds the right type of bacteria (mentioned previously) that produces no odor whatsoever. So, when the feces enters the tank, smells are immediately cut off as the bacteria goes to work converting the mess to compost. Because these bacteria break it down, it doesn't smell.

Reason #3: Separation of the liquids from the solids. Some toilets are "Urine Diverting Toilets" and never let the two mix in the first place, while some toilets such as the Sun-Mar units separate them once in the bin. It's really the urine/feces mix that causes nasty odors. It also separates the poop from the urine, controlling the moisture that can add excess smells and grow the bad kind of bacteria.

Produce a Finished Compost That is Safe and Easy to Handle

The last of the three core functions of a compost toilet is arguably the most important of them all. If modern compost toilet systems were unable to produce a safe to handle finished product, manufacturers would be right back to the drawing board!

Once a compost toilet's storage area is full, it will need to be emptied. This is the part of owning a compost toilet that makes most people a bit squeamish.

Understandably, handling human waste is not something we all get up in the morning looking forward to, but if your system is working properly, you should be handling a safe, nutrient rich soil, like garden compost, with no real signs of human waste to be seen or smelled.

Buying a system that is sized to your needs will help ensure very infrequent empties, like once or twice a year in some cases. This gives the system plenty of time to do its job and create a great additive for your flower garden or shrubs.

It's important to know your compost system. In some systems, a fully composted end product does not happen in the toilet itself due to size or design of the unit. In systems like these, having an outside compost pile to move the partially composted waste to is essential and the last part of the breakdown process happens there, not in the toilet at all.

A Step Further

Regardless of the type of toilet you get, they all work in similar ways. Each toilet is designed so that the chamber's environment is manipulated to allow for quick, odor free decomposition. It's this living ecosystem which transforms the waste into usable compost. Just like with any ecosystem, the conditions must be perfect inside the chamber for the bacteria to survive.

Composting toilets use several means to control the environment inside the chamber. With fans, separation trays, heating elements, and evaporation chambers, the system ensures only the right amount of moisture exists inside the chamber. Too much moisture will create some all too familiar odors and too little moisture will slow or even stop the decomposition process.

CHAPTER 3 - Things to Consider When Buying a Toilet

In this section, we want to run down a lot of the considerations you should make before buying

a composting toilet, all the different uses, and what you can expect. This section should answer

most of your questions if you have any.

Are composting toilets mobile for use in RVs, boats, or tiny homes?

The answer is YES…. And NO. Wait… What?

I know, that sounds tricky, but the real answer is it depends. Some composting toilets are

actually designed specifically to be used in mobile situations while others are very poorly suited

to life on the road.

Travel ready toilets have to overcome a few challenges that other compost toilets do not. Such

as being able to handle violent motion or jarring without being damaged, and in that same

environment, be able to contain the waste inside without splashing, spilling, or leaking.

While a lot of people use composting toilets for their environmental benefits, mobile ready

composting toilets are a little different. These are designed mostly for convenience while on the

road. They are often powered by 12 volt systems or in some cases with an internal battery that can be recharged with your typical 120-volt power source, but the charge lasts a good while. Non-electric versions are also available for the truly off-grid mobile toilet users.

Climate Considerations

There is a certain amount of heat that does happen during the composting process because microorganisms generate energy while doing their work. But the temperature inside the chamber does matter when it comes to how quickly they do work in converting feces into fertilizer. Every living organism has their optimum preferred climate where they thrive the best. If you live in a colder climate, it can slow down the growth of the bacteria and the entire conversion process. As long as the temperature inside the chamber is at least 55 degrees, composting will happen.

Most modern homes do not get below that threshold, so you should be fine in storing the composting toilet anywhere in the house, including the basement. These guidelines are mostly for outdoor or outhouse use. A lot of people use composting toilets in places with no running water, like off-the-grid homes, pole barns, or workplaces out of the way from a flush toilet, so consider the use you have in mind as well as the climate where it'll be used/stored.

If the temperature falls below the 50-55 degree Fahrenheit point, don't fret. Once the temp comes back up again, the composting process will begin right where it left off. Extended periods of time below 50 degree could mean waste will not break down as fast and more cleanouts will be required. It could also mean the waste being removed is not fully composted and will need to be moved to a remote compost pile to finish breaking down.

Does a Composting Toilet Meet Zoning Requirements?

There is no set rules or laws that apply to everyone across the country (meaning no national building laws that would apply). Each building code and standard is set by the individual counties, municipalities, and states. You can find your local guidelines with a simple Google search, but it's always best to ask your local zoning board before purchasing.

In the strictest locations, one popular brand of compost toilet has gone as far as obtaining the NSF certifications allowing it to be installed where others might not be welcome!

More often than not, it's not an issue of a specific ban on composting toilets but rather a blank stare when asked about them because they have simply not heard of them before. Being educated on the matter and presenting information to share will go a long way to getting approved from zoning officials.

If you're unsure of where to look, call your local or county government. They should also know the state laws regarding building as well.

Centralized or Self Contained Systems?

There are really two different types of compost toilet systems.

Self-Contained Systems

Self-contained compost toilet systems are fully functional compost toilet systems that act as the toilet and the composting chamber all in one. The come in electric and non-electric versions. In self-contained units, the waste is contained in the chamber at the base of the toilet, so the whole process takes place right there.

Several styles of self-contained composting toilet systems exist and for several different applications. From permanent home use to compact, mobile, space saving solutions. there's a pretty good chance a self-contained compost toilet exists for your needs.

Centralized System

Centralized systems have a separate composting unit somewhere else in the house or property. This is most like a traditional toilet, but instead of waste being flushed into the sewer or septic tank, the refuse is sent to this separate holding and composting container. The two are connected using a pipe or special adaptor tube, depending on the model.

Being that the centralized type of composting toilet is most like a traditional toilet, there are some that use water to help transport waste when a straight drop to the bin is not possible.

The toilets used on these systems are low flush toilets similar to those found in campers and RVs and use as little as one pint of water to flush waste into the composting chamber. For those without access to running water AND no direct drop to the composting chamber, there are even dry versions, and versions which use vacuum to suck the waste into the compost chamber!

Centralized systems allow for a much larger composting container which in turn allows for much longer times between cleanouts, larger number of people are able to use them, and compost has even more time to fully decompose making this type of system the most effective at producing fully decomposed, ready to use compost from human waste.

Urine diverting vs Non-Urine Diverting Composting Toilets

To maintain just the right amount of moisture in the composting chamber for proper decomposition and to cut down on odor, there are two different ways the composting toilet deals with liquid waste versus solid waste. Let's take a quick look at these options.

A urine diverting toilet has a different set up that collects the urine before it's ever mixed with solid waste. The urine is simply diverted (given the name) to the outlet where it's released into safe disposing area, like a container or proper drainage. This helps to ensure proper moisture levels in the composting area are maintained and eliminates the need to evaporate off additional moisture.

A non-diverting composting toilet simply separates the liquid from the solid once in the composting chamber. Some use a screen or mesh to separate while others use heat and air movement to evaporate excess moisture.

Separating the feces from the urine is essential to keeping the waste from turning into sewage and developing horrid smells. In the non-diverting systems, liquids enter the same area as the solids but are immediately separated by a screen, a special sifter of sorts, or air movement and heat to avoid creating sewage.

Bulking Material for Composting Toilets

Some toilets require bulking material adding additional cost to operation. The bulking materials are mixed in with the solid waste, which is why it's so important to turn the crank to mix it all together. This helps break apart the waste, allowing necessary oxygen to flow over and through the waste, speeding up the decomposition process.

It's best to consult the manufacturer or user manual before buying bulking material to ensure it would have no ill effect on the system. In addition, some bulking materials from big box stores can have dormant bug larva in it. The way to keep them from entering the system and infesting the chamber is by microwaving it for 30-45 seconds to kill off any eggs or larva.

What about Toilet Paper/Tissue?

Unlike RVs and camper toilet systems, there is no need to buy special toilet tissue for composting toilets. Any old TP will do!

Composting toilets do a great job of breaking down any toilet tissue you toss in right along with the human waste.

DO NOT however deposit feminine products into the composting toilet. These items do not breakdown well or quickly and will reduce the storage capacity of the system causing more frequent need of maintenance and cleanouts.

Will I Have to Deal with Worms, Flies, and Other Bugs?

You'd think having a storage tank in your home full of human waste would draw in the critters, but they really don't. Most insects, bugs, and even rodents are attracted by their sense of smell and since there is no odor. The majority of composting toilet users have no problems whatsoever with insects.

Although, there is an exception to every rule. Some users who have decided to shovel dirt, wood chips, peat, and/or any other type of organic material from their own backyard into the chamber as bulking material had issues with insects. They had no idea the material contained insect eggs/larvae, which hatched and invaded their operation.

There are also a few examples of flies getting into the chamber if/when the fan is turned off for several days, but if the fan is left on, the constant moving of air being sucked through will prevent any of that from happening.

How Do I Clean the Bowl?

Anyone who has ever used your average flush toilet knows that sometimes it can get a little messy. Maybe a little poop gets on the bowl and/or sticks to the porcelain. Because of this, most owners have plenty of bleach and a toilet brush to help keep things clean and sanitary. So, what happens with a composting toilet? What's the best way to clean the bowl?

You might think a composting toilet is much more unsanitary due to the lack of water and the flushing of waste, but a composting toilet is less like a toilet/bowl and more like pit. You have your typical toilet seat which sits on top of the container. After a few uses, you are fairly certain to hit the right spot to keep any mess from happening to begin with.

Still, we all want to make sure our toilet stays clean and sanitary. Most composting toilet users have a small spray bottle with a vinegar and water or baking soda and water mix for any sanitation needs. Simply spray and wipe. Do try to avoid too much spraying to keep added moisture out of the system.

Also, always avoid any household cleaners. It's tempting to spray store bought cleaners on the toilet to get it good and clean and kill those pesky germs. Unfortunately, this also kills the needed bacteria that are working so hard to break down the waste in the container!

Can I Compost Other Organic Materials in the Toilet?

The simple answer is yes you can, but NO you shouldn't. Manufacturers designed composting toilets for human waste. By adding anything extra, you are diminishing the capacity of the toilet and must empty and maintain it more often. Use an outside composter for other organic materials and you will extend the use time between empties dramatically.

By extending the time between empties, you are also allowing the waste to breakdown more fully. If you decrease the time between empties by adding other materials to the system, you will most likely be dealing with less than fully composted human waste when you DO empty the toilet.

CHAPTER 4 - What Toilet Is Right For Me?

As the human race continues to work on finding more environmentally friendly alternatives to the way we currently do things, more attention will be given to these types of items. More and more people are looking for ways to not only cut down on pollution, but to also save money while getting off the grid.

As more people learn about composting toilets, their popularity is growing. They have even become more acceptable and mainstream here in the USA which has been a HUGE hurdle for compost toilet manufacturers in the past decade.

In this book we have covered what a composting toilet is, how they work, and some common things to consider when purchasing one, now let's take a closer look at what options are on the market, and how to make the best decision when making your purchase!

Unlike most competitive markets, purchasing a compost toilet is more about features and requirements than it is about brand loyalty. In order to make your purchasing decision a little easier, we've gathered the top ten factors that sway a purchase decision one way or another and rated each of the popular brands.

Here are the ten most important things to look at when making your purchase decision...

- Ease of Install and maint.
- Self-contained or centralized.
- Mobile ready?
- Number of users.
- How often it needs emptied.
- Power requirements.
- Requires external liquid drain?
- Waste disposal and handling.
- Consumables required.
- Footprint or size of the system.

You'll notice in our ten most important purchasing comparisons, price is not listed. This was not omitted by accident, each system has advantages and disadvantages over other systems depending on its intended use and the price of each system reflects that accordingly. In other words, you pay for what you need!

Now that we have all that out of the way, let's get to the fun part and start shopping for the perfect composting toilet system for YOUR needs.

Nature's Head Dry Composting Toilet

Nature's Head is one of the top innovators of composting toilets and is quickly taking over the #1 spot in the composting toilet market. Their urine-diverting dry toilet works as both a mobile and stationary unit. It's lightweight and doesn't take up very much room at all. It has been constructed using sturdy polyethylene and stainless steel hardware to be tough and survive everything you can throw at it (including those bumpy roads or life in the wild).

Nature's Head toilets are completely self-contained and are electric 12 volt (or 120 volt with optional transformer). It comes with a 2.2-gallon urine bottle, a fan, and will go nearly anywhere you need a toilet. It comes with a full 5-year guarantee and will require the installation of a 2" vent hose. With the urine bottle, you can mix the liquid waste with 8 parts water to 1 part urine for safe disposal in a flower bed, providing extra nutrients.

With the use of bulking agents to help break up the solid waste, the final product will be around 10% the size it used to be for easy composting. Also, Nature's Head has been designed to handle any traveling you might do, so feel free to take it with you on any trips. The one downside is the amount of time it might take to break down the compost.

Users sometimes buy a second solid waste bin or even an external composter to give the solids more time to fully compost.

Ease of Install and maint.	Handyman Level 2 out of 10
Self contained or centralized.	Self Contained
Mobile ready?	Yes
Number of users.	2 full time - 3 part time
How often it needs emptied.	At full time use, approx once a month. More often for the liquid bottle.
Power requirements.	12 volt DC. 120 volt transformer available
Requires external liquid drain?	No
Waste disposal and handling.	Dump into garbage or external compost pile to finish breaking down.
Consumables required.	Coco-Fiber or Peat Moss
Footprint or size of the system.	19" Wide x 19" Deep x 20" Tall

In terms of price, the Nature's Head sells for around $960 making it one of the most affordable toilets on the market.

Seperatt Villa

The Separett Villa is a urine-diverting toilet that's well suited for stationary applications, but simply plumbing the liquids drain to a suitable black water storage tank makes it fit right into any mobile application, such as in an RV or camper. That is why the Separett composting toilets are quickly gaining in popularity with the mobile and tiny home crowd.

The Villa toilet was designed to look and feel as close to a traditional toilet as possible to make it easier for new users to adapt to using it. It can be used with on-grid use, as well as AC/DC configurations for those who want to run it in a 12v environment. You will have to install a vent pipe for the removal of odors outside of the building.

As a company, Seperatt believes the composting should be done away from the interior of the home, so the urine is diverted to a greywater system, a soak-away, or a tank away from the unit. It also had a 'chimney' stack for odors to be released away from the bathroom as well. The solid waste falls into a drum you can rotate to keep the mess from building up and stacking.

When you're ready to remove the waste, and take it to your compost pile, you won't have to worry about handling the mess, as it uses biodegradable bags for you to move it from one place to the next.

Sun-Mar Excel

Sun-Mar's website claims that the Excel composting toilet is the bestselling unit in North America thanks to its simple, yet advanced reliable design. This toilet has a great capacity for composting with its self-contained Bio-drum that's been certified by the National Sanitation Foundation.

The Excel is very easy to clean and has a 2" vent. Even though it will handle fluids through evaporation, there is an emergency drain in the back of the unit in case of very heavy use or you plan on using it residentially.

Compared to the previously mentioned toilets, the Excel can go MUCH longer with more people using it before needing emptied. It's also very poorly suited for mobile situations, because the liquids tray on the bottom of the unit would splash or leak when in motion.

Sun-Mar also has popular "Compact", "Mobile", and "Centrex" models, because they bring different areas of use to light. The Centrex is a whole house toilet replacement, the Compact is smaller than the Excel, and the Mobile is great when on the move. If you're a mobile user and looking for a great toilet to use on the run, Sun-Mar's "Mobile" version was actually designed specifically with boats and RVs in mind and can take a beating.

Laveo by Dry Flush

The Laveo is a small toilet unit, weighing in at a tiny 26 pounds, but does everything you need it to do. Mostly used as a portable option, the Laveo has a full-sized toilet seat, is light, and is battery-powered. Despite not being your typical composting toilet, the Laveo makes its way onto this list due to its increasing popularity in the composting market. Its popularity is growing thanks to its small size and method of keeping you from having to touch the raw waste.

Once you finish your business, you can 'flush' the toilet, sending the mess into a double-layered bagging system. When the bag is full, it seals itself and you can simply throw it away. You do not need any electricity, water, venting, or chemicals. You can recharge the Laveo with a 12-volt charger that comes with the toilet to work the bagging system.

For the reasons listed above, the Laveo's popularity with the RV and mobile crowd has been skyrocketing. It's simpler to just throw away the bag of waste than most of the other methods they use to dispose it. The downside is, if you're environmentally conscience, these cartridges can get expensive, costing $.75 per flush, and they do not compost. Once you throw them out, they end up in a landfill.

BioLet

BioLet toilets have all the look and feel of a traditional flush toilet, but has none of the issues. Made in Sweden, BioLet brand toilets are manufactured with leading state-of-the-art technology that knows your every move. It's a completely closed system that does all the work for you.

The moment you sit down on the seat, the trap door opens to allow the refuse to fall through into the chamber. Once you stand up and lift the seat, the toilet will do the mixing itself without forcing you to use the crank to turn the material yourself.

This toilet has two chambers. The first is for non-composted material and the second is for collecting the compost. Once the second is full and ready to be removed, you will see an LED indicator light come on. There's also a fan that helps to circulate the warm air created by the heater also in the unit. If there's too much liquid detected, a second heater will automatically turn on to help it evaporate.

EcoJohn BASIC

The EcoJohn Basic is in the same league as The Loveable Loo (below), as it's a very basic toilet, but takes its style and approach up a notch. Where the Loo is essentially a bucket with a toilet seat attacked, the EcoJohn looks just like a normal flush toilet and will separate liquid waste from the solid like a composting toilet.

This separation will cut down on the potential odor and bug issues that can come with the Loo-style toilets. Since they do not compost inside the chamber, certain smells might be prevalent, but with the EcoJohn, it has a vent to help that problem even further, as well as a heating plate to quickly dry out the solid waste.

The EcoJohn BASIC comes in two different models: the 12-volt and 120-volt options. This waterless toilet is another smart toilet that does a lot of the work for you. It separates the liquid and solid waste, sending the liquid through a waste hose and to a drain pit. The solids drop into what's called a 'waste box' that's lined with a bag, so you won't have to touch or handle any of it.

Under this box is a heating plate unit which works by drying the feces and raising the temperature to a degree that kills off most types of bacteria. As the box fills, you can easily pull the box and bag out and toss it into the compost. The bag and waste will both decompose.

The Loveable Loo

The Loveable Loo is a permanent wooden toilet for either indoor or outdoor use and is VERY simple to use. In fact, it's probably the simplest of all the toilets out there (and the cheapest!). It's essentially a 5-gallon bucket inside a wooden box with a toilet seat covering the hole. There's no use of electricity, plumbing, chemicals, venting, or water with this one.

It doesn't even require urine separation, but a lot of users end up modifying the Loo to fit their needs, adding a fan or urine separating toilets, which is one of its highlights. It's so easy to build, modify, and maintain that it remains one of the bestselling units on the market today. But its simplicity does have some drawbacks.

Because the Loveable Loo is little more than a bucket with a seat, it doesn't have the other benefits you'll find with a composting toilet. In fact, it's not a composting toilet at all. It takes the same basic idea and ingredients (for preventing smells), but will require you to empty the bucket in a separate compost bin. Which means you MUST have a compost bin to store it.

It's also not too aesthetically pleasing. You might not have a problem with the way it looks, but your guests might be a little weary of giving it a chance. And even when you use organic material to scoop inside the chamber, it might still end up smelling after prolonged use.

Santerra Green

The Santerra Green works just like the type of toilet you're used to, but much cleaner. One model uses a vacuum to suck the refuse as far as 70 feet away, where others use what's called a Micro-flush, which requires only about 7 ounces of water. It has a comfortable porcelain design that is sleek and looks exactly like an ordinary toilet.

The composting unit does all the work at turning the waste into compost and only has to be emptied maybe once or twice per year. It also has a 4" Wind Turbine fan to help treat the compost and keep the smells at bay. With this toilet, you won't have to worry too much about it breaking, as it comes with a 5-year warranty on all internal parts.

To power the Santerra Green, you can get it in three different modes, AC electric, 12-volt non-electric, and nonelectric, although it's recommended you use AC as it will provide the best performance.

In Conclusion

As environmental concerns continue to dominate the headlines, there's no doubt we'll continue to find new and innovative ways to change the way we do things for the better. It's up to each of us to make small changes for the betterment and the health of our planet. As the water crisis continues to heat up, we'll start to realize how important clean water is, not just to us individually, but for the other many billions of people we share the earth with.

A small change, like purchasing a compostable toilet, will have a cumulative overall impact, saving many thousands of gallons of clean drinking water per person each year. Not only will it save water (and your wallet), there will be many others around you who will feel inspired to follow in your footsteps.

More and more the trend seems to be heading back towards sustainable, off-the-grid living, but with numerous technological advantages our ancestors never could've imagined. The advent of solar panels, electric cars, and compostable toilets mean we can still enjoy modern comforts while saving our planet from ruin.

Made in the USA
Lexington, KY
10 September 2017